DOOR DESIGN

daab

Architects/Designers	Project	
Introduction		4
5+1AA Femia Peluffo	Wyler Vetta exhibition stand | Basilea	16
Andrés Jaque Arquitectos	Casa Sacerdotal Diocesana de Plasencia	20
Andrés Jaque Arquitectos	Tupper Home | Madrid	26
Andrew Maynard Architects	Essex Street House | Melbourne	30
Architectenbureau Paul de Ruiter	Villa Deys | Rhenen	36
Prof. Bernhard Hirche Dipl. Ing. Architekt BDA	House Buck | Hamburg	42
Architekturwerkstatt Matthias Loebermann	Exhibition building Baufritz | Erkheim	46
Architekturwerkstatt Matthias Loebermann	Paletten Pavillion | FH Biberach	52
Atelier Brückner	Thinktank | Stuttgart	58
Atelier Kempe Thill	IGA 2003 | Rostock	64
Atelier Kempe Thill	Concert hall Franz Liszt | Raiding	70
Atelier Kempe Thill	Terraced Houses | Roosendal	74
Behnisch und Partner mit Werner Durth	Akademie der Künste | Berlin	80
Bentel & Bentel Architects	The Modern | New York	84
Blocher Blocher Partners	BW Bank Stuttgart | Stuttgart	90
Bottega + Ehrhardt	Old indoor riding hall | Ludwigsburg	94
Bottega + Ehrhardt	House S | Stuttgart	98
Brückner & Brückner Architekten	Gambling House Bad Kissingen	102
Carola Schäfers Architekten BDA	FU Berlin, Centre for seminars, canteen II | Berlin	108
Ciel Rouge Création	Harajuku church | Tokyo	114
Architektengemeinschaft Zimmermann + Code Unique Architekten	New building for computing faculty of TU Dresden	118
Coll-Leclerc architects	Londres-Villarroel building | Barcelona	126
David Chipperfield	Museum of modern literature | Marbach am Neckar	130
Deffner, Voitländer Architekten	DV studio house | Dachau	136
Deffner, Voitländer Architekten	Primary school Augustenfeld | Dachau Augustenfeld	142
DUO PLAN Innenarchitektur + Architektur	Maisonette Apartment | Frankfurt	146
Bernhard Franken for ABB Architekten	BMW the bubble, Frankfurt Motor Show 99 | Frankfurt	150
Future Systems	255 Comme des Garçons | New York	154
Future Systems	Hauer-King House | Cannonbury	160
Future Systems	Marni Milano | Milano	164
Georg • Scheel • Wetzel Architekten	Foundation for the Institute for the Blind | Regensburg	168
gmp von Gerkan, Marg und Partner neuform-Türenwerk	Jakob Kaiser House | Berlin	174
GfG / Gruppe für Gestaltung GmbH	Dental practice Dr. Mittag | Bremen	180
GfG / Gruppe für Gestaltung GmbH	Dental practice Dr. Pabst | Berlin	186

Architects/Designers	Project	
Graft	Loft Greimstrasse	Berlin	196
Griffin Enright Architects	Rustic Canyon Residence	Pacific Palisades	202
Guy Lafranchi Architect	House L	Bern	206
l'Invisible	Showroom Via Santa Sofia	Milano	212
J. Mayer H.	Town House Ostfildern	218
Jensen & Macy Architects	kalwall door, wingingwall	San Francisco	222
John Friedman Alice Kimm Architects, Inc.	LA Design Center	Los Angeles	226
Jutta Heinze Architektin	Evangelic Christian Community	Duisburg	232
Jutta Heinze Architektin	Crematorium Waldfriedhof	Duisburg	238
Marcio Kogan	Gama-Issa House	Sao Paulo	244
Kohlmayer Oberst Architekten	Private House	Bietigheim-Bissingen	250
Kohlmayer Oberst Architekten	FU Bozen	Brixen	256
Iwa Leyk Wollenberg Architects	Private apartment	Berlin	264
Lynch Eisinger Design	Nike ID Design Lab	New York	270
META Architectuurbureau	Sheltered Workshops MIN	Antwerpen	274
MGF Architekten	Parking garage	Heilbronn	280
mori:projects, Claudia Wald + Mark Phillips GbR	Hecht residence	Stuttgart	286
mori:projects, Claudia Wald + Mark Phillips GbR	EnBW co-office	Berlin	292
Neil M. Denari architects	Endeavor Talent Agency Screening Room	Beverly Hills	296
Nieberg Architect	House K	Lehrte	300
Nieberg Architect	House FW	Harsum	304
Olson Sundberg Kundig Allen Architects	Chicken Point Cabin	Northern Idaho	308
Peter Haimerl, Studio für Architektur	Studio Mimesis	Munich	314
Peter Haimerl, Studio für Architektur	ZK Maximiliansforum	Munich	318
Ute Piroeth	Reconstruction of an old factory	Cologne	322
Prof. Christoph Mäckler Architekten	Levi-Strauss grammar school	Berlin	326
Prof. Christoph Mäckler Architekten	Exhibition Hall Portikus	Frankfurt	332
Prof. Peter Haas Architekten	Private House	Stuttgart	336
Sam Trimble Design, Inc.	Lady M	New York	342
Sanaksenaho Arkkitehdit Oy	St. Henry's Ecumenical Art Chapel	Turku	346
SATIJNplus architects	Kruisherenhotel/Lobby at Langhaus	Maastricht	350
Shigeru Ban Architects	Glass Shutter House	Tokyo	356
Skylab Design Group	Nike Air Jordan Xxperience	Denver	362
vonM	House R	Steinheim	368
Marcel Wanders	Restaurant Thor	New York	372
Zaha Hadid	Hotel Puerta America	Madrid	378
Index		381
Imprint		384

INTRODUCTION

The door is the most essential component of a house. It is both a separating as well as an adjoining element and permits or prevents entering from an external area to the private interior. Doors are interfaces that are created to invite or reject, depending on the message that they are to convey to the outside world. Closed or open – doors keeps secrets that can make you curious, awaken positive expectations or can also invoke your fears. Although the entrance in the most cases is also the exit, both are generally experienced in different manners. While the entrance can lead to unfamiliar territory, exiting a house is always a return to a familiar environment as well.

Throughout the entire history of architecture, doors have been adorned with mystical impressions from religion, superstition as well as art and literature history. In the Christian world, the fiery dragon swallows the souls of the damned as the "porta inferi". The dark gateway opens the entrance to the underworld and only a narrow portal leads to the Gates of Heaven. In the architecture of the monarchy, the entrance door was mostly the middle axis of a symmetrical building which increased the representative effect. The number of doorways which had to crossed marked the status of a potentate. Thus petitioners were obliged to wait for long periods in numerous reception rooms before they were able to present their requests.

Since then, doors have become a vivid component of our language. We live "door-to-door" with people, have "opened the door" to something and in an extreme case, matters can be discussed "behind closed doors". In our daily dealings, for example in the working world or in our private living space, there is hardly a part of a building that we have in our hands more often than the door handle. The entire scale of modern design can be interpreted on the basis of the development of this element. Oversized and heavy doors and gates to public buildings can often only be opened with a great deal of effort in order to create a certain amount of distance. Store entrances on the other hand allow prospective customers to cross their thresholds with little or no effort and are sometimes opened as if by magic.

In addition to the optical and tactile appeals, doors also offer acoustic experiences. Just as with constructing automobiles, it is a symbol of solidity and high quality when the door closes with a rich, powerful tone. Transparent or hermetically sealed doors – the material, the technology and the design create the spatial "calling card" of a house. Doors are far more than just "movable barriers by which an entry is closed or opened" as they are referred to in specialized literature. They are projection areas for our desires and make up the character of facades and interiors.

Die Tür ist der wichtigste Bestandteil eines Hauses. Sie ist sowohl trennendes als auch verbindendes Element zugleich und erlaubt oder verhindert das Eintreten vom Außenraum zum privaten Inneren. Türen sind Schnittstellen, die einladend oder abweisend gestaltet sind, je nachdem, welche Botschaft sie nach aussen kommunizieren sollen. Verschlossen oder offen – Türen verbergen Geheimnisse, die neugierig machen, positive Erwartungen wecken oder auch Ängste schüren können. Obgleich der Eingang in den meisten Fällen auch der Ausgang ist, wird beides in der Regel auf unterschiedliche Weise erlebt. Während das Eintreten auf noch unbekanntes Terrain führen kann, ist das Verlassen eines Hauses immer auch eine Rückkehr in ein bereits bekanntes Umfeld.

In der gesamten Baugeschichte wurden Türen mit mystischen Vorstellungen aus Religion, Aberglauben sowie der Kunst- und Literaturgeschichte belegt. Im christlichen Weltgericht verschlingt der Höllendrache als „porta inferi" die verdammten Seelen. Das dunkle Tor öffnet den Zugang zur Unterwelt und nur eine enge Pforte führt in das Himmelreich. In der Herrschaftsarchitektur lag die Eingangstür meist in der Mittelachse eines symmetrischen Baukörpers, was die repräsentative Wirkung steigerte. Die Anzahl der zu durchschreitenden Türen markierte den Status eines Potentaten. So waren Bittsteller genötigt, in den zahlreichen Vorzimmern, ausgiebig zu „antichambrieren" bevor sie ihr Anliegen vorbringen konnten.

Türen sind mittlerweile zu einem bildhaften Bestandteil unserer Sprache geworden. Wir leben Tür an Tür, uns haben sich Tor und Tür geöffnet und im Extremfall ist man mit der Tür ins Haus gefallen. Es gibt kaum ein Bauteil, das wir im alltäglichen Umgang beispielsweise in der Arbeitswelt oder in unserem privaten Wohnumfeld öfter in die Hand nehmen, als einen Türgriff. Schon allein anhand der Entwicklung dieses Elements lässt sich die gesamte Skala des modernen Design ablesen. Großformatige und schwere Türen und Tore zu öffentlichen Bauten lassen sich oft nur mit erheblichem Kraftaufwand öffnen, um eine gewisse Distanz zu vermitteln. Ladentüren hingegen lassen den möglichen Kunden mit möglichst geringer Anstrengung seine Schwellenangst überwinden und öffnen sich manchmal wie von Geisterhand bewegt von selbst.

Neben optischen und haptischen Reizen bieten Türen auch akustische Erlebnisse. So ist es, ähnlich wie im Automobilbau, ein Zeichen von Solidität und Hochwertigkeit, wenn die Tür mit einem satten Ton ins Schloss fällt. Transparente oder hermetisch dichte Türen - das Material, die Technik und das Design prägen die räumliche Visitenkarte eines Hauses. Türen sind weit mehr als „bewegliche Raumabschlüsse", wie es in der technischen Fachliteratur heißt. Sie sind Projektionsflächen für unsere Wünsche und prägen den Charakter von Fassaden und Innenräumen.

La puerta es el componente más importante de la casa. Un elemento que por una parte separa y por otra une los diversos espacios permitiendo o impidiendo la entrada del exterior al espacio interior privado. Las puertas son puntos de intersección diseñados de forma acogedora o bien hostil dependiendo del mensaje que se quiera comunicar hacia el exterior. Cerradas o abiertas, las puertas albergan secretos que estimulan la curiosidad, crean expectativas positivas e incluso suscitan temor. Y aunque por lo general la entrada es a su vez la salida de la vivienda, ambas se suelen experimentar de forma diferente. Mientras que la entrada frecuentemente conduce a un espacio interior aún desconocido, la salida de una vivienda siempre es también un retorno a un ámbito ya familiar.

En toda la Historia de la Construcción se han asociado las puertas a las ideas místicas de la religión y la superstición, así como de la Historia del Arte y de la Literatura. En el juicio final cristiano, por ejemplo, el dragón del infierno enguye las almas condenadas a modo de "porta inferi". La oscura puerta representa la entrada al infierno, y sólo una estrecha puerta conduce al reino de los cielos. En la arquitectura de palacios y edificios gubernamentales, la puerta de entrada solía encontrarse en el eje central de un edificio simétrico, lo que incrementaba el efecto representativo del mismo. El número de puertas que había que pasar marcaba el estatus del potentado. De este modo, los súbditos se veían obligados a esperar en las antesalas antes de poder presentar sus peticiones.

Las puertas se han convertido en una expresión figurativa de nuestra lengua. Vivimos puerta a puerta, a veces se nos abren todas las puertas y en casos extremos nos tiran la puerta abajo. Por otra parte, casi ningún elemento constructivo se utiliza tanto en la vida cotidiana, en el mundo laboral y en el ámbito privado como el picaporte de la puerta. Observando tan sólo la evolución que ha experimentado este elemento vemos la amplia variedad que ofrece el diseño moderno. Con frecuencia se requiere bastante fuerza para abrir las grandes y pesadas puertas que conducen a los edificios públicos, porque con ello se pretende crear cierta distancia. En cambio, las puertas a establecimientos comerciales se abren sin ninguna dificultad con objeto de ayudar al potencial cliente a superar su inicial resistencia a la nueva situación que se le plantea al entrar en la tienda, y a veces incluso se abren automáticamente como por arte de magia.

Junto a los estímulos visuales y hápticos que nos transmiten las puertas, suscitan sensaciones acústicas. De modo similar a los automóviles, se considera una señal de solidez y alta calidad que la puerta se cierre con un sonido sonoro. El material, la tecnología y el diseño de las puertas –ya sean éstas transparentes o de cierre hermético– representan la tarjeta de visita espacial de una casa. Las puertas son mucho más que meros "elementos móviles de separación de espacios", como se califican en la bibliografía técnica. Son superficies de proyección de nuestros deseos, y determinan el carácter de las fachadas y de los espacios interiores.

La porte est l'élément le plus important d'une maison. Elle est cette paroi qui à la fois sépare et unit, elle permet ou interdit de quitter l'espace extérieur, public, pour pénétrer dans l'intimité du foyer. Les portes sont des interfaces, elles peuvent être d'un aspect accueillant ou au contraire dissuasif, ceci suivant le message que l'on veut leur faire communiquer au monde extérieur. Qu'elles soient fermées ou ouvertes, les portes cachent des secrets qui aiguisent la curiosité, elles éveillent des attentes positives mais peuvent aussi inspirer de la peur. Bien que l'entrée serve, dans la plupart des cas, également de sortie, le fait d'entrer et de sortir est généralement vécu de manière différente. Tandis qu'entrer peut signifier se rendre sur un terrain inconnu, quitter une maison signifie toujours revenir dans un environnement familier. Dans toute l'histoire de la construction, les portes ont été assorties de représentations mythiques empruntées à la religion, à la superstition, mais aussi à l'histoire de l'art et à celle de la littérature. Dans le tribunal chrétien du Jugement Dernier, le dragon symbolisant la « porte des enfers » engloutit les âmes damnées. Une porte sombre ouvre accès aux enfers et à la pègre, et seule une petite porte étroite permet d'entrer au paradis. Dans l'architecture patricienne, la porte d'entrée se situe généralement sur l'axe médian d'un bâtiment aux contours symétriques, ceci dans le but d'accroître l'effet d'élégance et de puissance. Par le passé, le nombre de portes à franchir marquait également le statut social du potentat. Ainsi les solliciteurs étaient-ils contraints de patienter dans les nombreuses antichambres avant de pouvoir exposer leur requête.

Dans l'intervalle, les portes forment partie intégrante et imagée de notre langue. On parle de faire du porte à porte, de mettre quelqu'un à la porte ou de lui claquer la porte au nez. Il n'est guère d'objet, dans un bâtiment, que nous ne prenions plus souvent en main – dans l'accomplissement des gestes quotidiens, au travail par exemple ou dans notre environnement résidentiel privé – qu'une poignée de porte. Déjà rien que le développement de cet élément est à lui seul un livre ouvert dans lequel se lit toute l'évolution du design moderne. Les portes et portails lourds et de grande taille donnant accès aux bâtiments publics ne se laissent ouvrir qu'au prix d'un effort important, et marquent ainsi une certaine distance par rapport à celui qui veut y pénétrer. Inversement, les portes de magasin ne demandent qu'un effort minime au client potentiel, pour lui faire surmonter son appréhension, et s'ouvrent parfois d'elles-mêmes, comme si une main invisible les actionnait.

Outre leur charme visuel et leurs agréables retours haptiques, les portes sont aussi synonymes d'expériences auditives. Ainsi par exemple, et ceci vaut également pour la construction automobile, une porte entrant avec un bruit mat mais ferme en contact avec la serrure est un signe de robustesse et de haute qualité. Portes transparentes ou portes étanches : les matériaux et techniques mobilisés ainsi que le design caractérisent la carte de visite spatiale que laisse une maison. Les portes sont bien plus que des « délimitations mobiles de l'espace » comme le suggèrent les ouvrages spécialisés. Les portes sont ces surfaces sur lesquelles nous projetons nos aspirations ; elles participent au cachet des façades et annoncent celui des pièces intérieures.

La porta rappresenta l'elemento più importante della casa e – contemporaneamente separando e collegando – permette o impedisce l'accesso dall'ambiente esterno verso gli spazi privati interni. Le porte sono interfacce create in modo invitante o respingente, secondo il messaggio che vogliono comunicare all'esterno. Chiuse o aperte – le porte talvolta nascondono segreti che stuzzicano la curiosità, suscitano aspettazioni o incutono paura. Anche se spesso l'entrata funge da uscita, l'effetto delle due risulta diverso. Mentre l'entrata può portare verso un mondo sconosciuto, l'uscita dalla casa è sempre anche un ritorno in un ambiente già noto.

In tutta la storia dell'architettura, alle porte sono state attribuite idee e misticismi della religione e la superstizione, della storia dell'arte e della letteratura. Nel Giudizio universale, la furia infernale come "porta inferi" divora le anime condannate. L'oscuro portone apre l'accesso verso gli inferi e soltanto uno stretto sportello porta al Paradiso. Nell'architettura feudale, spesso la porta d'entrata si trovò sull'asse centrale di una costruzione simmetrica, aumentando così l'effetto rappresentativo. Il numero di porte da attraversare indicava l'alta posizione del potentato, obbligando i postulanti a "fare anticamera" nelle numerose sale d'attesa prima di poter rivolgere le loro petizioni.

Ormai le porte sono diventate un elemento immaginifico del ns. linguaggio. Abitiamo porta a porta con qualcuno, gli spalanchiamo le porte e, nel caso estremo, sfondiamo porte aperte. Nella nostra vita quotidiana di lavoro o privata in casa, non esiste quasi nessun altro elemento così spesso toccato con le mani come la maniglia delle porte. Lo sviluppo di questa componente fa capire tutta la scala del design moderno. Ampie e pesanti porte e portoni degli edifici pubblici sovente si aprono soltanto con grande sforzo, per rendere l'idea di una certa distanza da rispettare. Le porte dei negozi invece aiutano il cliente a superare con il minore sforzo possibile una sua eventuale esitazione di entrare e, certe volte, come guidate da mani invisibili le porte si aprono da sole.

Oltre ad attrattive visive e tattili, le porte regalano anche sensazioni acustiche. Così, analogo alle automobili, si considera segno di solidità ed alta qualità quando la serratura della porta si chiude con un suono pieno. Porte trasparenti o ermetiche – il loro materiale, la tecnica ed il design formano il biglietto da visita della casa. Porte sono molto più che sole "chiusure mobili di vani" come indicherebbe il termine tecnico. Rappresentano la superficie su cui proiettiamo i ns. desideri e che impregna il carattere di facciate ed ambienti interni.

5+1AA FEMIA PELUFFO | GENOVA
Wyler Vetta exhibition stand
Basilea, Switzerland | 2003
Photos: Ernesta Caviola

ANDRÉS JAQUE ARQUITECTOS | MADRID
Casa Sacerdotal Diocesana de Plasencia
Plasencia, Spain | 2004
Photos: Miguel de Guzmán

ANDRÉS JAQUE ARQUITECTOS | MADRID
Tupper Home
Madrid, Spain | 2006
Photos: Miguel de Guzmán

ANDREW MAYNARD ARCHITECTS | MELBOURNE
Essex Street House
Melbourne, Australia | 2005
Photos: Peter Bennetts

ARCHITECTENBUREAU PAUL DE RUITER | AMSTERDAM
Villa Deys
Rhenen, Netherland | 2002
Photos: Alessio Guarino

PROF. BERNHARD HIRCHE DIPL. ING. ARCHITEKT BDA | HAMBURG
House Buck
Hamburg, Germany | 1996
Photos: Gert von Bassewitz, Oliver Heissner

ARCHITEKTURWERKSTATT MATTHIAS LOEBERMANN | NÜRNBERG
Exhibition building Baufritz
Erkheim, Germany | 2005
Photos: Mila Hacke

ARCHITEKTURWERKSTATT MATTHIAS LOEBERMANN | NÜRNBERG
Paletten Pavillion
FH Biberach, Germany | 2005
Photos: Mila Hacke

ATELIER BRÜCKNER | STUTTGART
Thinktank
Stuttgart, Germany | 2001
Photos: Katharina Feuer

ATELIER KEMPE THILL | ROTTERDAM
IGA 2003
Rostock, Germany | 2003
Photos: Architektur-Fotografie Ulrich Schwarz

ATELIER KEMPE THILL | ROTTERDAM
Concert hall Franz Liszt
Raiding, Austria | 2006
Photos: Architektur-Fotografie Ulrich Schwarz

ATELIER KEMPE THILL | ROTTERDAM
Terraced houses
Roosendal, Netherlands | 2005
Photos: Architektur-Fotografie Ulrich Schwarz

BEHNISCH UND PARTNER MIT WERNER DURTH | STUTTGART
Akademie der Künste
Berlin, Germany | 2005
Photos: Christian Kandzia, Esslingen

BENTEL & BENTEL ARCHITECTS | NEW YORK
The Modern
New York, New York, USA | 2004
Photos: Eduard Huber, Arch Photo, Inc.

BLOCHER BLOCHER PARTNERS | STUTTGART, MANNHEIM
BW Bank Stuttgart
Stuttgart, Germany | 2006
Photos: Courtesy of Blocher Blocher View

BOTTEGA + EHRHARDT | STUTTGART
Old indoor riding hall
Ludwigsburg, Germany | 2000
Photos: David Franck Photographie

BOTTEGA + EHRHARDT | STUTTGART
House S
Ludwigsburg, Germany | 2002
Photos: David Franck Photographie

BRÜCKNER & BRÜCKNER ARCHITEKTEN | TIRSCHENREUTH/WÜRZBURG
Gambling House Bad Kissingen
Bad Kissingen, Germany | 2005
Photos: Constantin Meyer, Köln; Peter Manev, Selb

CAROLA SCHÄFERS ARCHITEKTEN BDA | BERLIN
FU Berlin, Centre for seminars, canteen II
Berlin, Germany | 2006
Photos: Stefan Müller, Berlin

CIEL ROUGE CRÉATION | PARIS, TOKYO
Harajuku church
Tokyo, Japan | 2005
Photos: Toshihisa Ishii

**ARCHITEKTENGEMEINSCHAFT ZIMMERMANN
+ CODE UNIQUE ARCHITEKTEN | DRESDEN**
New building for computing faculty of TU Dresden
Dresden, Germany | 2006
Photos: Courtesy of AG Zimmermann + Code Unique

COLL-LECLERC ARCHITECTS | BARCELONA
Londres-Villarroel building
Barcelona, Spain | 2006
Photos: Jose Hevia

DAVID CHIPPERFIELD | LONDON
Museum of Modern Literature
Marbach am Neckar, Germany | 2006
Photos: Jörg von Bruchhausen, Wilfried Dechau

DEFFNER, VOITLÄNDER ARCHITEKTEN | DACHAU
DV studio house
Dachau, Germany | 2005
Photos: Courtesy of Deffner, Voitländer Architekten,
Prof. Dieter Leistner

DEFFNER, VOITLÄNDER ARCHITEKTEN | DACHAU
Primary school Augustenfeld
Dachau Augustenfeld, Germany | 2006
Photos: Courtesy of Deffner, Voitländer Architekten,
Prof. Dieter Leistner

DUO PLAN INNENARCHITEKTUR + ARCHITEKTUR | FRANKFURT
Maisonette Apartment
Frankfurt, Germany | 2005
Photos: Frank Herrmann

BERNHARD FRANKEN FOR ABB ARCHITEKTEN | FRANKFURT
BMW the bubble, Frankfurt Motor Show 99
Frankfurt am Main, Germany | 1999
Photos: Friedrich Busam

FUTURE SYSTEMS | LONDON
255 Comme des Garçons
New York, USA | 1998
Photos: Richard Davies

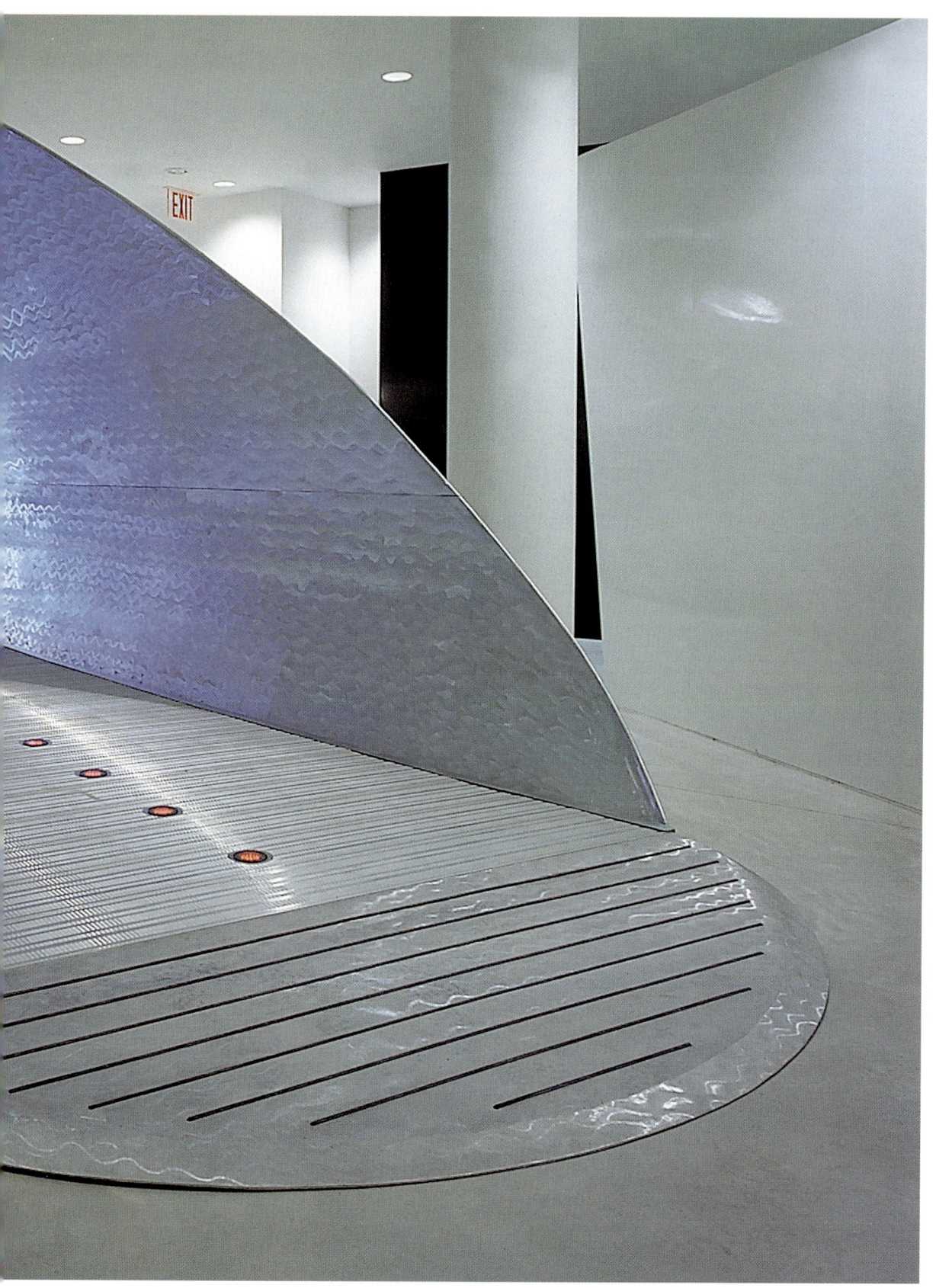

FUTURE SYSTEMS | LONDON
Hauer-King House
Cannonbury, UK | 1992
Photos: Richard Davies

FUTURE SYSTEMS | LONDON
Marni Milano
Milano, Italy | 1999
Photos: Richard Davies

GEORG • SCHEEL • WETZEL ARCHITEKTEN | BERLIN
Foundation for the Institute for the Blind
Regensburg, Germany | 2005
Photos: Stefan Müller, Berlin

GMP VON GERKAN, MARG UND PARTNER | HAMBURG
NEUFORM-TÜRENWERK | ERDMANNHAUSEN
Jakob Kaiser House
Berlin, Germany | 2001
Photos: Jörg F. Müller, Berlin

GFG / GRUPPE FÜR GESTALTUNG GMBH | BREMEN
Dental practice Dr. Mittag
Bremen, Germany | 2005
Photos: Thomas Kleiner / GfG

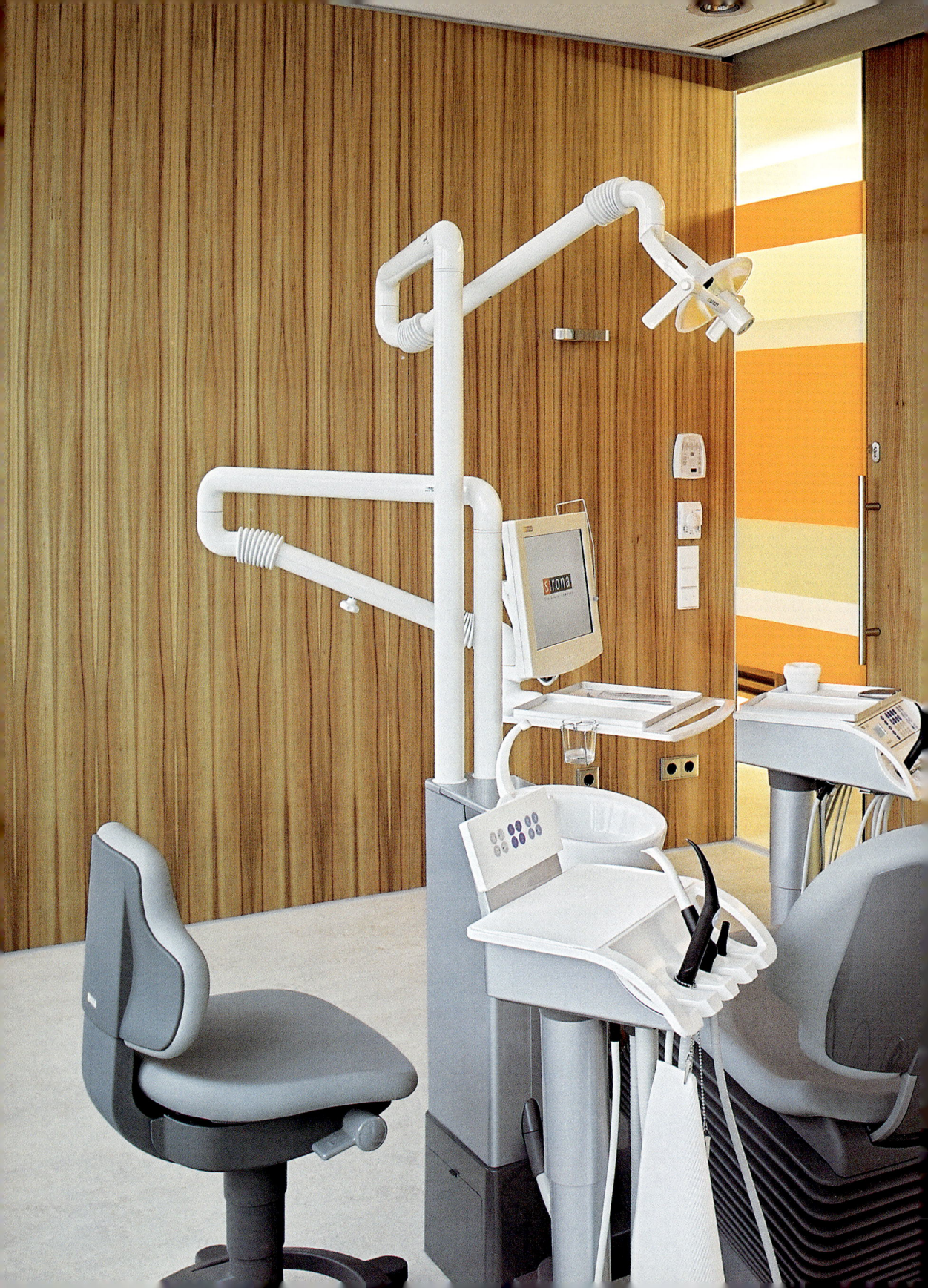

GFG / GRUPPE FÜR GESTALTUNG GMBH | BREMEN
Dental practice Dr. Pabst
Berlin, Germany | 2002
Photos: Thomas Kleiner / GfG

GRAFT | BERLIN, LOS ANGELES
Loft Greimstrasse
Berlin, Germany | 2004
Photos: Jan Bitter, Berlin

GRIFFIN ENRIGHT ARCHITECTS | LOS ANGELES
Rustic Canyon Residence
Pacific Palisades, CA | 2001
Photos: Art gray, AMC Photograghy

GUY LAFRANCHI ARCHITECT | BERN
House L
Bern, Switzerland | 1998
Photos: Angelo Kaunat

Doors [R]evolution

L'INVISIBLE | ARGENTA
Showroom Via Santa Sofia
Milano, Italy | 2005
Photos: Enrico Colzani

J. MAYER H. | BERLIN
Town House Ostfildern
Ostfildern, Germany | 2001
Photos: David Franck Photograph

JENSEN & MACY ARCHITECTS | SAN FRANCISCO
kalwall door, wingingwall
San Francisco, USA | 2004
Photos: Richard Barnes

JOHN FRIEDMAN ALICE KIMM ARCHITECTS, INC. | LOS ANGELES
LA Design Center
Los Angeles, USA | 2004
Photos: Benny Chan, Fotoworks

JUTTA HEINZE ARCHITEKTIN | DUISBURG
Evangelic Christian Community
Duisburg, Germany | 2005
Photos: Tomas Riehle

JUTTA HEINZE ARCHITEKTIN | DUISBURG
Crematorium Waldfriedhof
Duisburg, Germany | 2002
Photos: Tomas Riehle

MARCIO KOGAN | SAO PAULO
Gama-Issa House
Sao Paulo, Brasil | 2001
Photos: Arnaldo Pappalardo

KOHLMAYER OBERST ARCHITEKTEN | STUTTGART
Private House
Bietigheim-Bissingen, Germany | 2004
Photos: Günter Richard Wett, Innsbruck

KOHLMAYER OBERST ARCHITEKTEN | STUTTGART
FU Bozen
Brixen, Italy | 2004
Photos: Günter Richard Wett, Innsbruck

LWA LEYK WOLLENBERG ARCHITECTS | BERLIN
Private apartement
Berlin, Germany | 2005
Photos: diephotodesigner.de, Berlin

LYNCH EISINGER DESIGN | NEW YORK
Nike ID Design Lab
New York, USA | 2005
Photos: Lynch Eisinger Design, Paul Warchol Photography

META ARCHITECTUURBUREAU | ANTWERPEN
Sheltered Workshops MIN
Antwerpen, Belgium | 2004
Photos: Sarah Blee

MGF ARCHITEKTEN | STUTTGART
Parking garage
Heilbronn, Germany | 1998
Photos: Courtesy of MFG Architekten

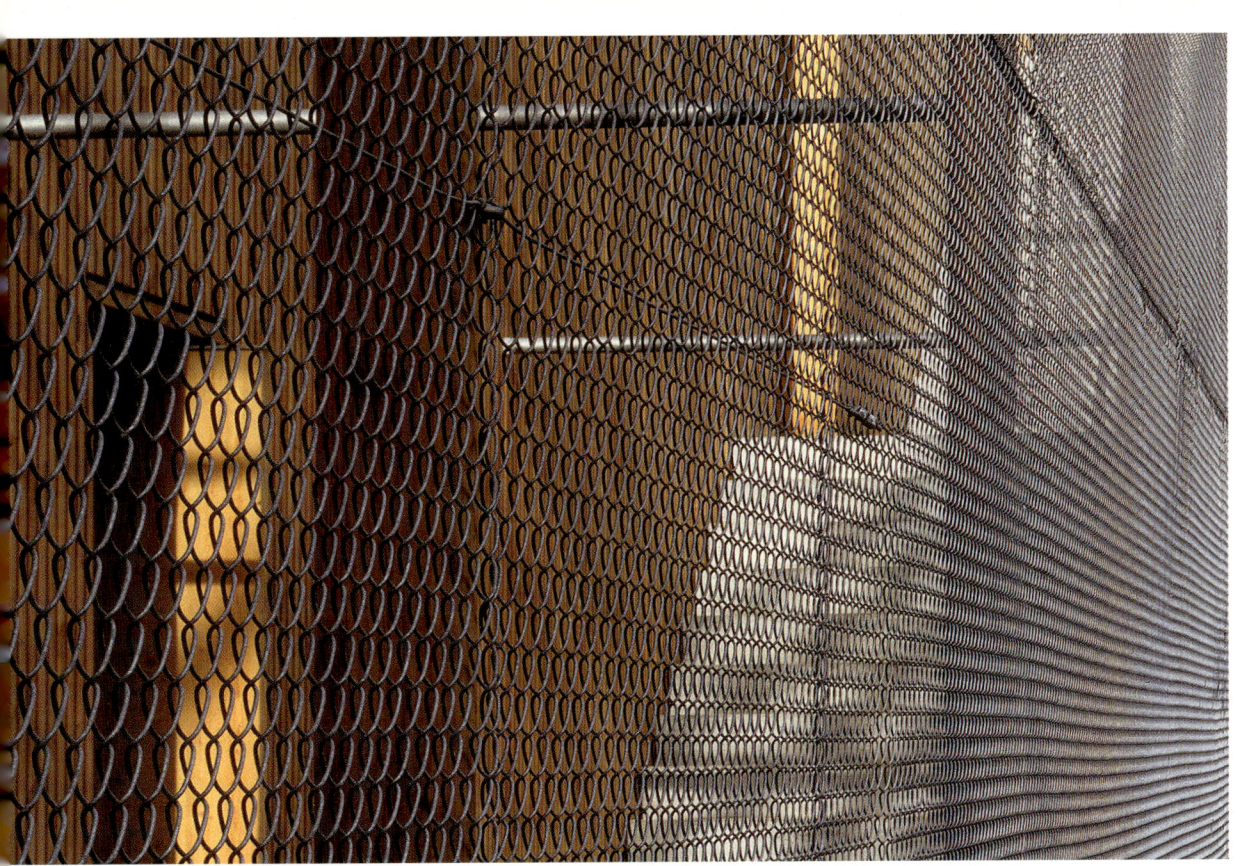

MORI:PROJECTS | STUTTGART
Hecht Residence
Stuttgart, Germany | 2005
Photos: Peter Thiede

MORI:PROJECTS | STUTTGART
EnBW co-office
Berlin, Germany | 2005
Photos: Fritz Busam

NEIL M. DENARI ARCHITECTS | LOS ANGELES
Endeavor Talent Agency Screening Room
Beverly Hills, CA | 2004
Photos: Benny Chan, Fotoworks

NIEBERG ARCHITECT | HANNOVER
House K
Lehrte, Germany | 2004
Photos: Axel Nieberg

NIEBERG ARCHITECT | HANNOVER
House FW
Harsum, Germany | 2004
Photos: Axel Nieberg

OLSON SUNDBERG KUNDIG ALLEN ARCHITECTS | SEATTLE
Chicken Point Cabin
Northern Idaho, USA | 2003
Photos: Benjamin Benschneider

PETER HAIMERL, STUDIO FÜR ARCHITEKTUR | MUNICH
Studio Mimesis
Munich, Germany | 1994
Photos: Angelo Kaunert

PETER HAIMERL STUDIO FÜR ARCHITEKTUR | MUNICH
ZK Maximiliansforum
Munich, Germany | 2006
Photos: Edward Beierle

UTE PIROETH | COLOGNE
Reconstruction of an old factory
Cologne, Germany | 2001
Photos: Bernd Michael Maurer

PROF. CHRISTOPH MÄCKLER ARCHITEKTEN | FRANKFURT
Levi Strauss grammar school
Berlin, Germany | 2002
Photos: Chistoph Lison, Frankfurt

PROF. CHRISTOPH MÄCKLER ARCHITEKTEN | FRANKFURT
Exhibition Hall Portikus
Frankfurt, Germany | 2006
Photos: Chistoph Lison

PROF. PETER HAAS ARCHITEKTEN | STUTTGART
Private House
Stuttgart, Germany | 1993
Photos: Katharina Feuer

SAM TRIMBLE DESIGN, INC. | NEW YORK
Lady M
New York, USA | 2005
Photos: Paul Warchol Photography

SANAKSENAHO ARKKITEHDIT OY | HELSINKI
St. Henry's Ecumenical Art Chapel
Turku, Finland | 2005
Photos: Jussi Tiainen, Helsinki

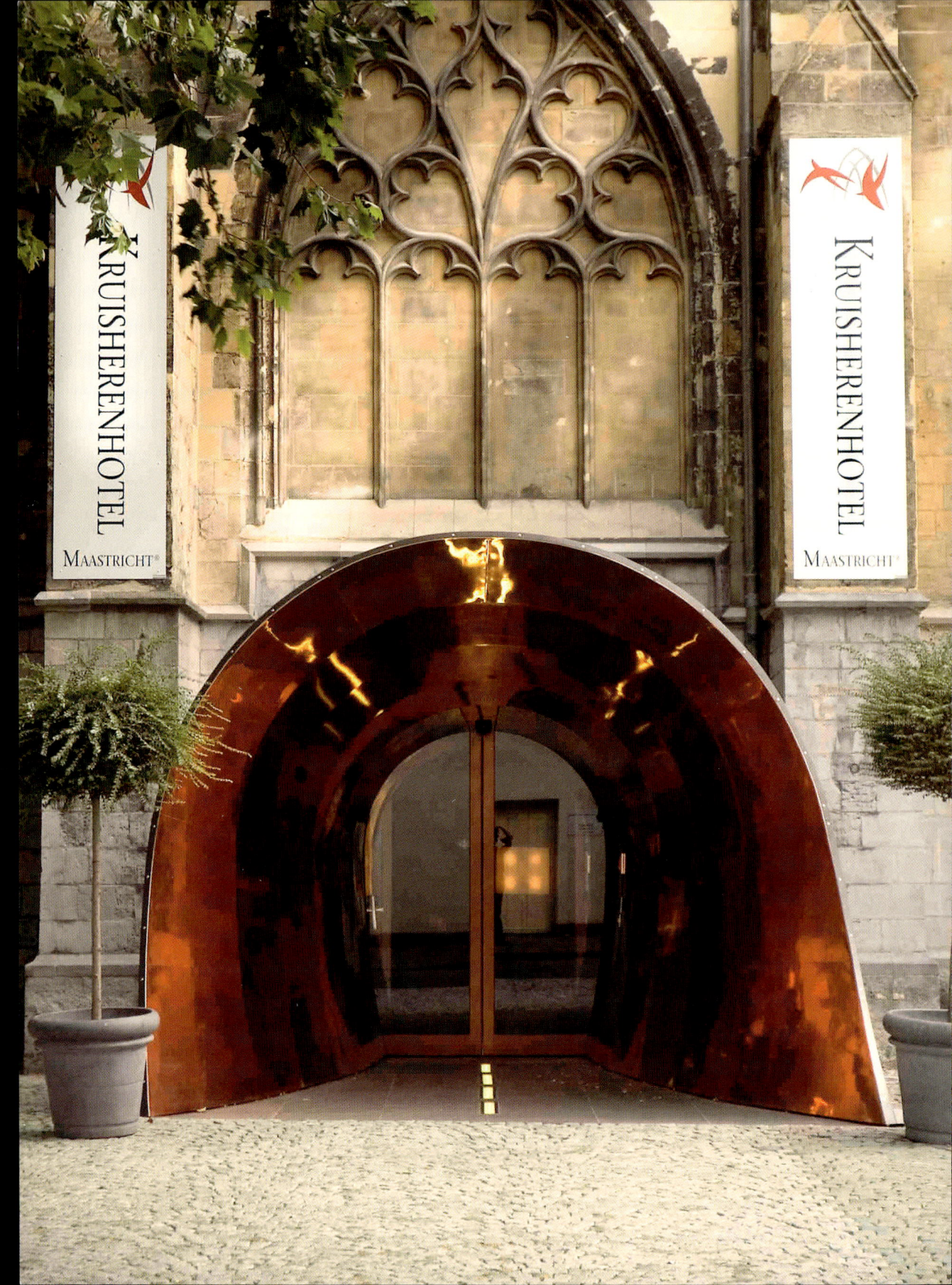

SATIJNPLUS ARCHITECTS | BORN
Kruisherenhotel / Lobby at Langhaus
Maastricht, Netherland | 2005
Photos: Etiënne van Sloun, Luc Boegly

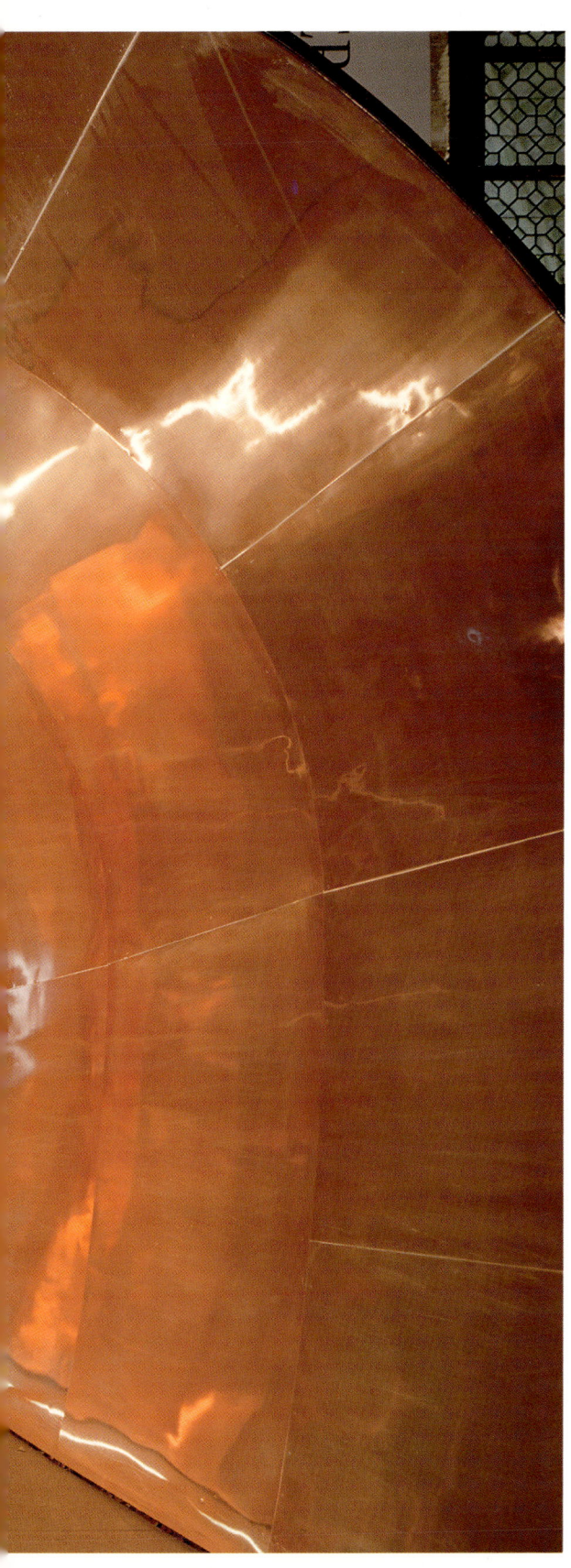

SHIGERU BAN ARCHITECTS | TOKYO
Glass Shutter House
Tokyo, Japan | 2003
Photos: Hiroyuiki Hirai

SKYLAB DESIGN GROUP | PORTLAND
Nike Air Jordan Xxperience
Denver, Colorado, USA | 2005
Photos: Shaun Jarvis

VONM | STUTTGART
House R
Steinheim, Germany | 2005
Photos: Boris Wiechulla, Stuttgart

MARCEL WANDERS | AMSTERDAM
Restaurant Thor
New York, USA | 2005
Photos: Inga Powilleit

ZAHA HADID | LONDON
Hotel Puerta America
Madrid, Spain | 2005
Photos: Silken Hotels Group , Helene Binet

INDEX

5+1AA Femia Peluffo | Genova
www.5piu1aa.com
Wyler Vetta exhibition stand | Basilea — 16
Photos: Ernesta Caviola

Andrés Jaque Arquitectos | Madrid
www.andresjaque.net
Casa Sacerdotal Diocesana de Plasencia | Placencia — 20
Tupper Home | Madrid — 26
Photos: Miguel de Guzmán

Andrew Maynard Architects | Melbourne
www.andrewmaynard.com.au
Essex Street House | Melbourne — 30
Photos: Peter Bennetts

Architectenbureau Paul de Ruiter | Amsterdam
www.paulderuiter.nl
Villa Deys | Rhenen — 36
Photos: Alessio Guarino

Prof. Bernhard Hirche Dipl. Ing. Architekt BDA | Hamburg
House Buck | Hamburg — 42
Photos: Gert von Bassewitz (doors),
Oliver Heissner (hall)

Architekturwerkstatt Matthias Loebermann | Nürnberg
www.aml-partner.de
Exhibition building Baufritz | Erkheim — 46
Paletten Pavillion | FH Biberach — 52
Photos: Mila Hacke

Atelier Brückner | Stuttgart
www.atelier-brueckner.de
Thinktank | Stuttgart — 58
Photos: Katharina Feuer

Atelier Kempe Thill | Rotterdam
www.atelierkempethill.com
IGA 2003 | Rostock — 64
Concert hall Franz Liszt | Raiding — 70
Terraced Houses | Roosendal — 74
Photos: Architektur-Fotografie Ulrich Schwarz

Behnisch und Partner mit Werner Durth | Stuttgart
www.behnisch.de
Akademie der Künste | Berlin — 80
Photos: Christian Kandzia, Esslingen

Bentel & Bentel Architects | New York
www.bentelandbentel.com
The Modern | New York — 84
Photos: Eduard Huber, Arch Photo, Inc.

Blocher Blocher Partners | Stuttgart
www.blocherblocher.com
BW Bank Stuttgart | Stuttgart — 90
Photos: Courtesy of Blocher Blocher View

Bottega + Ehrhardt | Stuttgart
www.be-arch.com
Old indoor riding hall | Ludwigsburg — 94
House S | Stuttgart — 98
Photos: David Franck Photographie

Brückner & Brückner Architekten | Tirschenreuth, Würzburg
mail@architektenbrueckner.de
Gambling House | Bad Kissingen — 102
Photos: Constantin Meyer, Köln; Peter Manev, Selb

Carola Schäfers Architekten BDA | Berlin
www.csa-berlin.de
FU Berlin, Centre for seminars, canteen II | Berlin — 108
Photos: Stefan Müller, Berlin

Ciel Rouge Création | Tokyo
www.cielrouge.com
Harajuku church | Tokyo — 114
Photos: Toshihisa Ishii

Architektengemeinschaft Zimmermann + Code Unique Architekten | Dresden
www.ag-zimmermann.de
www.codeunique.de
New building for computing faculty of
TU Dresden | Dresden — 118
Photos: Courtesy of AG Zimmermann + Code Unique

Coll-Leclerc architects | Barcelona
www.coll-leclerc.com
Londres-Villarroel building | Barcelona — 126
Photos: Jose Hevia

David Chipperfield | London
www.davidchipperfield.co.uk
Museum of modern literature | Marbach am Neckar — 130
Photos: Jörg von Bruchhausen, Wilfried Dechau (p 130)

Deffner, Voitländer Architekten | Dachau
www.dv-arc.de
DV studio house | Dachau — 136
Primary school Augustenfeld | Dachau Augustenfeld — 142
Photos: Courtesy of Deffner, Voitländer Architekten,
Prof. Dieter Leistner (p 138, 139, 145)

DUO PLAN Innenarchitektur + Architektur | Frankfurt
www.duo-plan.de
Maisonette Apartment | Frankfurt 146
Photos: Frank Herrmann

Bernhard Franken for ABB Architekten | Frankfurt
www.franken-architekten.de
BMW the bubble, Frankfurt Motor Show 99 | Frankfurt 150
Photos: Friedrich Busam

Future Systems | London
www.future-systems.com
255 Comme des Garçons | New York 154
Hauer-King House | Cannonbury 160
Marni Milano | Milano 164
Photos: Richard Davies

Georg • Scheel • Wetzel Architekten | Berlin
www.georgscheelwetzel.com
Foundation for the Institute for the Blind | Regensburg 168
Photos: Stefan Müller, Berlin

gmp von Gerkan, Marg und Partner | Hamburg
www.gmp-architekten.de
neuform-Türenwerk | Erdmannhausen
www.neuform-tuer.de
Jakob Kaiser House | Berlin 174
Photos: Jörg F. Müller, Berlin

GfG / Gruppe für Gestaltung GmbH | Bremen
www.gfg-bremen.de
Dental practice Dr. Mittag | Bremen 180
Dental practice Dr. Pabst | Berlin 186
Photos: Thomas Kleiner / GfG

Graft | Berlin, Los Angeles
www.graftlab.com
Loft Greimstrasse | Berlin 196
Photos: Jan Bitter

Griffin Enright Architects | Los Angeles
www.griffinenrightarchitects.com
Rustic Canyon Residence | Pacific Palisades 202
Photos: Art Gray, AMC Photograghy

Guy Lafranchi Architect | Bern
www.guylafranchi.ch
House L | Bern 206
Photos: Angelo Kaunat

l'Invisible | Argenta
www.linvisibile.it
Showroom Via Santa Sofia | Milano 212
Photos: Enrico Colzani

J. Mayer H. | Berlin
www.jmayerh.de
Town House Ostfildern | Ostfildern 218
Photos: David Franck Photograph

Jensen & Macy Architects | San Francisco
www.jensen-macy.com
kalwall door, wingingwall | San Francisco 222
Photos: Richard Barnes

John Friedman Alice Kimm Architects, Inc. | Los Angeles
www.jfak.net
LA Design Center | Los Angeles 226
Photos: Benny Chan, Fotoworks

Jutta Heinze Architektin | Duisburg
www.juttaheinze.de
Evangelic Christian Community | Duisburg 232
Crematorium Waldfriedhof | Duisburg 238
Photos: Tomas Riehle

Marcio Kogan | Sao Paolo
www.marciokogan.com
Gama-Issa House | Sao Paulo 244
Photos: Arnaldo Pappalardo

Kohlmayer Oberst Architekten | Stuttgart
www.kohlmayer-oberst-architekten.de
Private House | Bietigheim-Bissingen 250
FU Bozen | Brixen 256
Photos: Günter Richard Wett, Innsbruck

Iwa Leyk Wollenberg Architects | Berlin
www.lwarchitects.de
Private apartment | Berlin 264
Photos: diephotodesigner.de, Berlin

Lynch Eisinger Design | New York
www.lwarchitects.de
Nike ID Design Lab | New York 270
Photos: Lynch Eisinger Design (p 270),
Paul Warchol Photography (p 273)

META Architectuurbureau | Antwerpen
www.meta-architectuur.be
Sheltered Workshops MIN | Antwerpen 274
Photos: Sarah Blee

MGF Architekten | Stuttgart
www.mgf-architekten.de
Parking garage | Heilbronn 280
Photos: Courtesy of MFG Architekten

mori:projects,
Claudia Wald + Mark Phillips GbR | Stuttgart
www.mori-projects.de
Hecht residence | Stuttgart 286
Photos: Peter Thiede
EnBW co-office | Berlin 292
Photos: Fritz Busam

Neil M. Denari architects | Los Angeles
www.nmda-inc.com
Endeavor Talent Agency
Screening Room | Beverly Hills 296
Photos: Benny Chan, Fotoworks

Nieberg Architect | Hannover
www.nieberg-architect.de
House K | Lehrte 300
House FW | Harsum 304
Photos: Axel Nieberg

Olson Sundberg Kundig Allen Architects | Seattle
www.olsonsundberg.com
Chicken Point Cabin | Northern Idaho 308
Photos: Benjamin Benschneider

Peter Haimerl, Studio für Architektur | Munich
www.urbnet.de
Studio Mimesis | Munich 314
Photos: Angelo Kaunat
ZK Maximiliansforum | Munich 318
Photos: Edward Beierle

Ute Piroeth | Cologne
www.piroeth-architektur.de
Reconstruction of an old factory | Cologne 322
Photos: Bernd Michael Maurer

Prof. Christoph Mäckler Architekten | Frankfurt
www.chm.de
Levi-Strauss grammar school | Berlin 326
Exhibition Hall Portikus | Frankfurt 332
Photos: Chistoph Lison, Frankfurt

Prof. Peter Haas | Stuttgart
Private House | Stuttgart 336
Photos: Katharina Feuer

Sam Trimble Design, Inc. | New York
www.samtrimble.com
Lady M | New York 342
Photos: Paul Warchol Photography

Sanaksenaho Arkkitehdit Oy | Helsinki
www.personal.eunet.fi/pp/sanaks/HomeUK.htm
St. Henry's Ecumenical Art Chapel | Turku 346
Photos: Jussi Tiainen, Helsinki

SATIJNplus architects | Born
www.satijnplus.nl
Kruisherenhotel / Lobby at Langhaus | Maastricht 350
Photos: Etiënne van Sloun (p 350, 352),
Luc Boegly (p 353, 354)

Shigeru Ban Architects | Tokyo
www.shigerubanarchitects.com
Glass Shutter House | Tokyo 356
Photos: Hiroyuiki Hirai

Skylab Design Group | Portland
www.skylabdesign.com
Nike Air Jordan Xxperience | Denver 362
Photos: Shaun Jarvis

vonM | Stuttgart
www.vonm.de
House R | Steinheim 368
Photos: Boris Wiechulla, Stuttgart

Marcel Wanders | Amsterdam
www.marcelwanders.com
Restaurant Thor | New York 372
Photos: Inga Powilleit

Zaha Hadid | London
www.zaha-hadid.com
Hotel Puerta America | Madrid 378
Photos: Silken Hotels Group (p 378),
Helene Binet (p 380)

© 2007 daab
cologne   london   new york

published and distributed worldwide by
daab gmbh
friesenstr. 50
d-50670 köln

p + 49 - 221 - 913 927 0
f + 49 - 221 - 913 927 20

mail@daab-online.com
www.daab-online.com

publisher ralf daab
rdaab@daab-online.com

creative director feyyaz
mail@feyyaz.com

editorial project by fusion publishing gmbh stuttgart . los angeles
© 2007 fusion publishing, www.fusion-publishing.com

editor katharina feuer, jons messedat

layout katharina feuer
imaging digigra4, www.digigra4.de, susanne olbrich

photo credits
coverphoto courtesy of ag zimmermann + code unique
introduction page 7 courtesy of silken hotels, 9 katharina feuer, 11 david franck photograph,
13 fritz busam, 15 jose hevia
text introduction jons messedat
translations by ade team übersetzungen/stuttgart, claudia ade
english translation jill kaiser
french translation dominique santoro
spanish translation margarita celdràn-kuhl
italian translation jacqueline rizzo

printed in slovenia
www.mkt-print.com

isbn 978-3-937718-56-9

all rights reserved.
no part of this publication may be reproduced in any manner.